B *is for* bravo

Kevin Burgemeestre

KIPAS BOOKS

Introduction

B is for Bravo celebrates the first full century of human flight. Over 100 years, aircraft has evolved from gas balloons and the flimsy craft of sticks and string, to space shuttles that charge out into silent space.

Australians were connected to flight from the first toss of the boomerang. Perhaps because of the enormous distances within our land it was logical that flying would become a national obsession. The danger seemed to appeal to our larrikin, adventurous spirit. Pioneer aviators cheated death to discover air routes, many of which are still flown today.

Aircraft and radio developed side by side as logical partners in a shrinking world, and the phonetic alphabet was developed to help break through the crackles and buzzes that plagued early transmission. A curious list of words was chosen that would be easily understood by people of different nationalities. There are different versions of the phonetic alphabet and the NATO alphabet used in this book originated 1955. For example, the acronym NATO would be sounded out November, Alpha, Tango, Oscar.

I have illustrated this book using dioramas, in memory of the wonderful museums that have shown me the great things of the world in miniature. Carving and shaping each aircraft and holding them in my hands, gave me a much better appreciation of these magic and elegant fish of the air.

Kevin Burgemeestre

A is for ALPHA, ABORIGINAL and AEROFOIL

Alpha means first. The Aboriginal and Torres Strait Islander peoples were the first to use an aerofoil tens of thousands of years ago when they constructed boomerangs.

An aerofoil has a top surface that is more curved than the bottom, which causes it to rise as it moves through the air. Aerofoils are the basis of flight and are used in every aeroplane wing. They are also used in aircraft propellers and the rotors of helicopters.

They are used upside down on the racing cars, not to help them rise but to force them down onto the track and create grip.

B is for BRAVO and BALLOON

"Bravo!" we cry when balloonists rise above the earth using hot air and gas. Drifting with the wind means they can do without heavy, troublesome engines.

In 1782 the Montgolfier brothers stunned onlookers with the first manned balloon flight. Two passengers rose high above Paris in a huge hot air balloon, made of blue paper and silk.

76 years later, the first Australian balloon flew over the Yarra River in Melbourne piloted by Joseph Dean.

Thousands viewed the spectacular event, but promoter George Coppin lost money because most refused to pay admission to his fairground to see the flight begin. They easily viewed the 20 metre balloon as it rose above the grounds alongside the Yarra.

Australia had become part of the race for the skies.

Alpha | Bravo | Charlie

C is for CHARLIE and COURAGE

Charlie is Australian slang for a bit of a fool. Flying, at times, required both foolish and courageous acts.

Among the most courageous were competitors in the great air races. In 1919 brothers Keith and Ross Smith with mechanics Wally Shiers and Jim Bennett were the first to fly from England to Australia. This won them the 10,000 pound prize awarded by Australian Prime Minister Billy Hughes. Their aircraft was a converted, long range, Vickers Vimy bomber with open cockpits.

This tough plane and crew emerged from World War I. Aviation had progressed enormously and in the miracle of peace they were keen to tackle anything. Their journey took them over mountains, deserts, and dangerous seas. They survived fierce storms that blinded them and froze their wings, almost dropping them from the skies.

In Surabaya, when their plane became bogged after a heavy storm, all seemed lost. But villagers saved them by covering the mushy airstrip with bamboo mats from their own homes, allowing them to take off and reach Darwin to claim the prize. Sadly, four other competitors lost their lives during the race.

| Alpha | Bravo | Charlie | Delta | Echo |

D is for
DELTA and DINOSAURS

Delta is a triangular wing used in aircraft design. This dinosaur's wings have a similar shape.

Flight has existed on earth for millions and millions of years. Firstly seeds and insects took to the air and by the time of the dinosaurs huge creatures capable of flight had developed. The fossil records show Pterosaurs, with heads like darts and mouths full of sharp teeth, which cruised the skies on long slender wings. The largest Pterosaur discovered, Quetzalcoatlus, had a massive 12-metre wingspan. They were the largest organisms ever to have flown on our planet. That would have been something to see!

E is for ECHO and EXPLORE

Explorers undertaking expeditions to the unknown also hope to return, just like an echo.

In 1928 great explorer Sir Hubert Wilkins and co-pilot Ben Eielson were first to fly over the North Pole, establishing an air link between America and Europe. Wilkins had a strong belief in the ability of aircraft and a keen interest in the Polar Regions. He was a decorated hero, war correspondent, spy, pioneer cinematographer and one of the most remarkable men of the last century.

The Arctic flight required great courage because there could be no rescue for the men if they were forced down. They wore layers of furs, and flew with thick gloves in a cockpit that iced up from the cold. When the engine stalled they managed to land on dangerous, fractured sea ice without crashing. They repaired the engine in conditions so cold they could lose fingers to frostbite. Totally exhausted, Sir Hubert struggled to free the aircraft from the grip of the ice and clamber aboard the aircraft on a rope ladder, while Eielson kept the engine running. Twice Sir Hubert fell and the aircraft took off without him. Luckily, he was successful on his third attempt!

Alpha | Bravo | Charlie | Delta | Echo | Foxtrot

F is for
FOXTROT and FLYING DOCTORS

A Foxtrot is a quick dance with a partner. Flying doctors use planes to reach isolated places quickly to help the sick or injured.

Reverend John Flynn toured the outback in the 1920s and saw the hardship people faced living far from medical care. Death resulted from injuries that easily could have been treated in a hospital or with the help of a doctor. He pledged to obtain quality care for these forgotten people of the bush.

After lobbying politicians, his determination was rewarded in 1928 when he started the Flying Doctor Service with government funding. Where there was no electricity, pilots were alerted by the pedal radio.

They took extraordinary risks to land on bush airstrips, paddocks and and rough roads to reach patients.

Many country people tell amazing stories about how the Flying Doctor has saved their lives, and today it has grown to become one of Australia's most respected services.

Alpha | Bravo | Charlie | Delta | Echo | Foxtrot | Golf | Hotel

G is for GOLF and GLIDERS

Golf is a game where a ball is struck and travels through the air. Gliders travel through the air using the force of the wind.

In the late nineteenth century inventors used gliders to help solve important problems of lift and control. It was the last step before powered flight. The brilliant Otto Lilienthal in Germany designed and constructed gliders in which he made over 2,000 successful flights.

Australian Lawrence Hargrave devoted his life to developing a stable flying machine by experimenting with many box kites and gliders. He illustrated lectures in London by releasing models that flew above the heads of the astounded audience. Initially regarded as a bit of a joke in Australia, Hargrave's work won international respect and Australians now honour him as one of aviation's great pioneers.

Modern gliders are designed using the lightest and strongest materials to achieve enormous distances, even without power.

Otto Lilienthal

Lawrence Hargrave

H is for
HOTEL and HAZARDS

When a supersonic Concorde ploughed into a hotel near Paris in July 2000, it reminded us that even the most awesome planes face hazards, which can cause them to crash.

Aircraft designers work hard to learn from disaster and minimise risk. Australian scientist Dr David Warren, conceived the Black Box Flight Recorder to store flight data about in a box strong enough to withstand crashes.

Today all commercial aircraft carry a data recorder to retrieve information, pinpoint dangers and save lives. Curiously, the box is not black, but fluorescent orange so that it can be easily spotted, and it has round corners, so it is not really a box either!

| Alpha | Bravo | Charlie | Delta | Echo | Foxtrot | Golf | Hotel | India | Juliet |

I is for
INDIA and INSTRUMENTS

India is an important destination during transglobal flights. On long flights instruments become the pilots senses. Early pilots relied on their eyes, ears and noses for information. As journeys became longer more reliable information was needed.

Gyroscopic instruments changed flying completely. Pilots were trained to fly under completely hooded cockpits and rely on instruments more than their senses.

Radio made communication possible, and transmitted reliable homing beacons. Radar became a new tool that electronically warned of coming danger. These inventions made reliable long distance flight a reality.

Today, computers provide pilots with more information than ever. However modern glass screens show only what is essential while the autopilot flies the plane making constant adjustment to speed and course. Entire journeys can be made in our time without human hands touching the controls.

J is for JULIET and JETLINER

Juliet was Shakespeare's romantic heroine confined to her house and the church, waiting for Romeo.

Jetliners are powerful, large aircraft that can transport many people and big payloads over long distances with speed and safety. Aircraft like the Boeing 747 Jumbo jet have revolutionised travel by being able to carry up to 500 people 10,000 kilometres at speeds of 980 kilometres per hour.

This enables average families to reach distant and exotic places reasonably cheaply. In fact you may be on a plane right now, reading this book!

Migration has also increased as people use aircraft to seek opportunities around the globe. In Juliet's world families stayed in the same place for generations these days she would probably search for Romeo by boarding a jet!

Alpha | Bravo | Charlie | Delta | Echo | Foxtrot | Golf | Hotel | India | Juliet | Kilo | Lima

K is for
KILO and KINGSFORD SMITH

A kilo is a measure of weight. Aircraft have to be light and strong to perform well so aircraft designers save kilos where they can.

Charles Kingsford Smith or 'Smithy' became famous in 1928 when he and his crew were first to cross the Pacific Ocean from America to Australia. Smithy was an Aussie larrikin who fancied taking risks.

He had been a soldier at Gallipoli, a stunt pilot, and had even dangled from aeroplanes to make a living.

He was an excellent long-distance pilot, who set many records. Sadly, he and navigator Tommy Pethybridge, crashed off the coast of Burma in 1935. Their final fate remains a mystery.

L is for
LIMA and LIVES

Above Lima, capital of Peru, the vast wings of the condor sweep it to the peaks of the mighty Andes Mountains. Aircraft are a peak of 20th Century inventiveness, constantly shaping our lives.

After Cyclone Tracy hit Darwin in 1974, aircraft took away sick and injured people, and brought supplies to rebuild the city.

East Timor was a devastated after the struggle for independence and many lives were in danger. Australia was one of the nations anxious to help. In September 1999 Dili airport was repaired and a stream of aircraft arrived, like the large Lockheed Hercules, which carried heavy supplies and even vehicles into the city.

| Alpha | Bravo | Charlie | Delta | Echo | Foxtrot | Golf | Hotel | India | Juliet | Kilo | Lima |

M is for MIKE and MiG

A Mike is an instrument that picks up sounds electronically. Pilots use mikes to communicate.

MiG is a dangerous family of rugged Russian fighter planes, which originated in the 1940s. They form the aerial fighting force of many nations up to the present day. From the frozen Arctic through the sunbaked Middle East, down through Africa, they have stood against the air forces of many western nations.

In the early 1950s, at the start of the Korean War, Australian pilots encountered MiG jet fighters in out-of-date propeller driven Mustangs.

A number of veteran MiGs have been privately imported and occasionally can be seen cruising Australian skies.

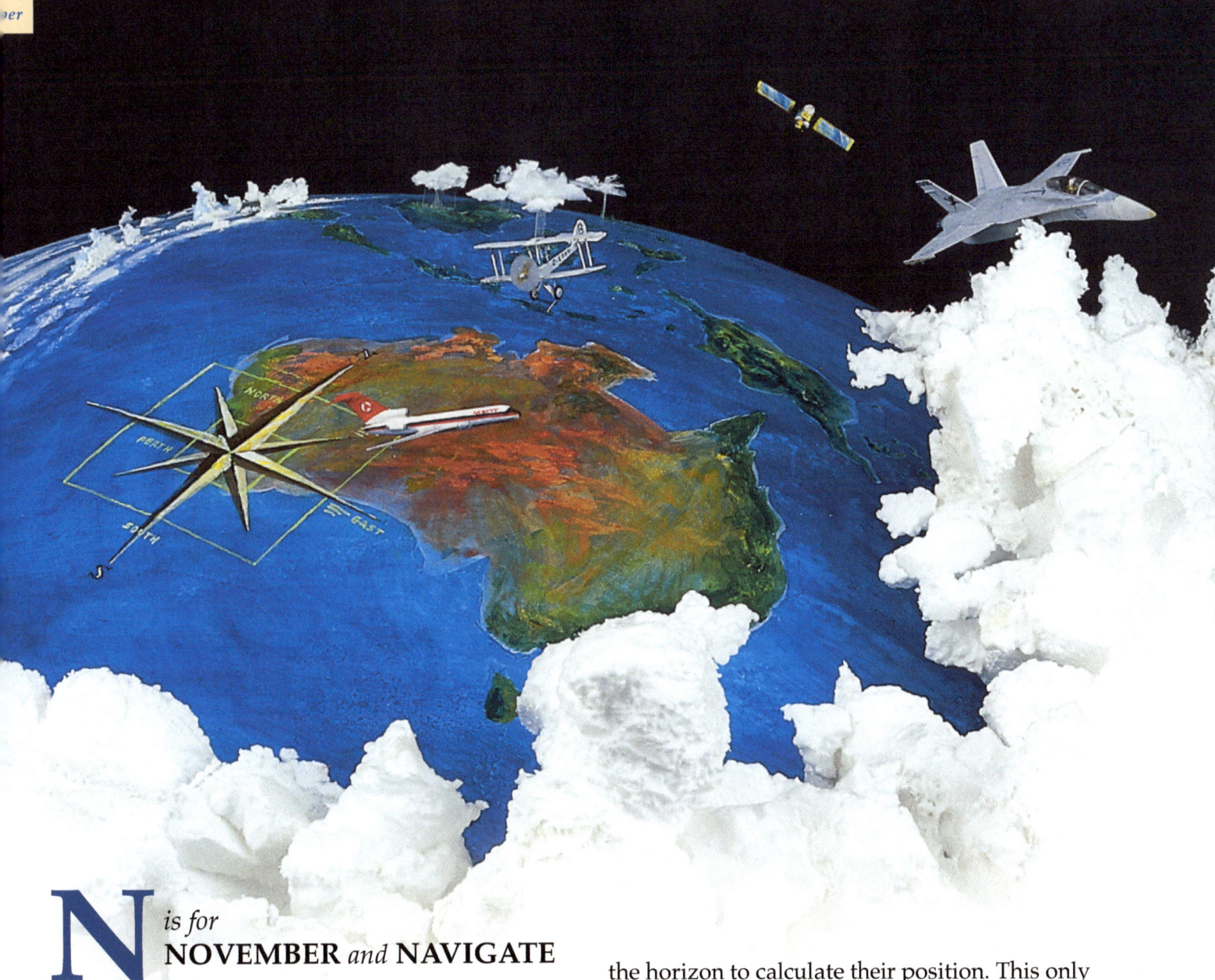

N is for
NOVEMBER and NAVIGATE

November directs us to the year's end, just as navigators direct travellers to their destinations.

Early pilots used the 'iron compass', a comical name for railway lines. They strapped a map to their knees and looked over the side of the cockpit to see where they were going.

On longer journeys pilots used a sextant to view the position of the stars or sun in relation to the horizon to calculate their position. This only worked when there were no clouds or rain.

Compasses based on spinning gyroscopes allowed precise and unwavering courses to be set. Radio beacons established during World War II could be picked up by aircraft radio receivers to establish position. This allowed the first long-distance airliners to navigate safely. Today computers and global positioning systems take the responsibility of finding the way.

| Alpha | Bravo | Charlie | Delta | Echo | Foxtrot | Golf | Hotel | India | Juliet | Kilo | Lima |

O is for OSCAR and OCEANS

Oscar is the name of the first American satellites used by ships to find their position at sea. Oceans cover two-thirds of the surface of planet earth.

Crossing the oceans was one of the biggest hurdles faced by aircraft. Huge oceans required large, heavy fuel loads and navigators needed to be precise to locate tiny islands in the vast seas. Because aircraft now regularly cross the ocean quickly and safely, they are the best way to rescue those in danger.

Ocean yacht racers are far from land and at the mercy of weather. Huge winds and massive waves can smash boats to pieces. Unable to move, sailors pray for the sound of helicopter rotors or the drone of aircraft engines, which mean brave pilots and crew are coming to rescue them.

| Alpha | Bravo | Charlie | Delta | Echo | Foxtrot | Golf | Hotel | India | Juliet | Kilo | Lima |

P is for PAPA and PHOTOGRAPHY

Papa is another word for father. The fathers of aerial photography used cameras mounted on hot air balloons to get panoramic views.

Aerial photos allow us to understand the world and show places difficult for humans to visit, like the tops of the highest mountains, inside volcano cones, and dangerous places like the Antarctic.

Aerial photography can be used to plan battles, but also to chart more efficient agriculture and living spaces, and such information as the migration of whales.

Astronauts looking down on the earth are astounded to find no evidence of the thousands of kilometres of borders we have created to separate countries. They just see a single planet that is home to us all.

Q is for QUEBEC and QANTAS

Quebec is a French-speaking city in Canada. A QANTAS jet could take you there.

QANTAS was one of the world's first airlines. It was registered in 1921 in Queensland by Paul J McGinness and Hudson Fysh, who had both fought in World War I, learned to fly, and been awarded medals for bravery.

The initials QANTAS stand for Queensland and Northern Territory Air Services. It began with two planes flying mail across the dusty north. Government-subsidised mail services helped start commercial aviation because they paid operators regular income while they gained experience.

The first paying passenger on a scheduled service was not carried until November 1922. He was 84 years old!

The operation grew and linked with British Imperial Airways in 1934 to create a regular service from Australia to England. Even during World War II, QANTAS served Australia heroically, moving people and equipment.

Today QANTAS is an international airline and the flying kangaroo is known throughout the world.

Alpha *Bravo* *Charlie* *Delta* *Echo* *Foxtrot* *Golf* *Hotel* *India* *Juliet* *Kilo* *Lima*

R *is for* ROMEO *and* RACING

Romeo is Shakespeare's hero who wins Juliet's heart. Racers compete to find a winner.

Racing encourages designers to seek creative solutions to make aircraft lighter and faster. Right from the start, pilots competed to see how far, fast and high their new aerial upstarts could go.

In 1903 the famous Wright Flyer from the USA led the way and became the first practical, controllable aircraft.

The first international aviation meeting was held at Rheims, France in 1909, where pilots and aircraft competed for prizes. Many records were determined and designers gathered information that improved aircraft design.

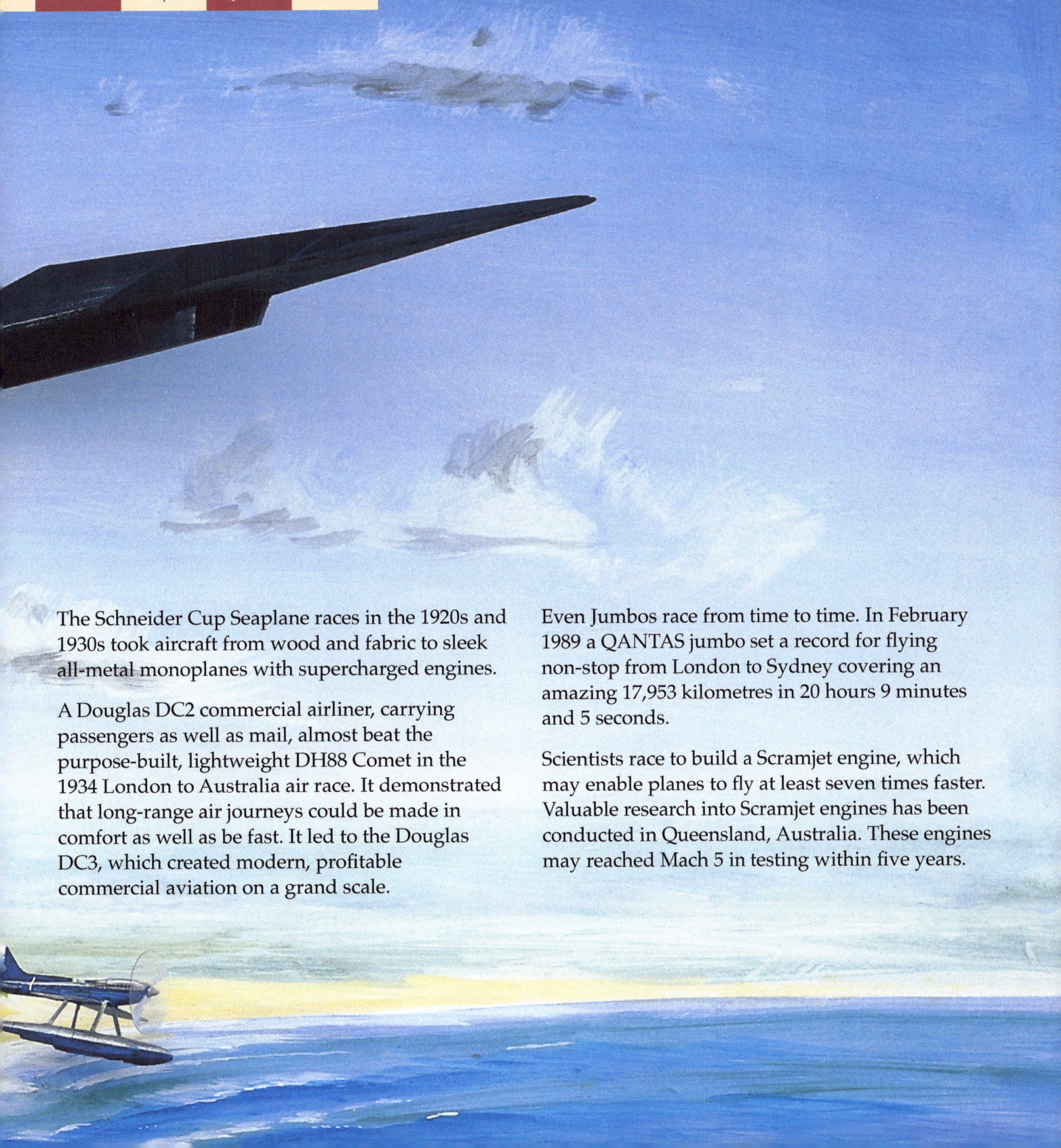

| ber | Oscar | Papa | Quebec | Romeo |

The Schneider Cup Seaplane races in the 1920s and 1930s took aircraft from wood and fabric to sleek all-metal monoplanes with supercharged engines.

A Douglas DC2 commercial airliner, carrying passengers as well as mail, almost beat the purpose-built, lightweight DH88 Comet in the 1934 London to Australia air race. It demonstrated that long-range air journeys could be made in comfort as well as be fast. It led to the Douglas DC3, which created modern, profitable commercial aviation on a grand scale.

Even Jumbos race from time to time. In February 1989 a QANTAS jumbo set a record for flying non-stop from London to Sydney covering an amazing 17,953 kilometres in 20 hours 9 minutes and 5 seconds.

Scientists race to build a Scramjet engine, which may enable planes to fly at least seven times faster. Valuable research into Scramjet engines has been conducted in Queensland, Australia. These engines may reached Mach 5 in testing within five years.

| Alpha | Bravo | Charlie | Delta | Echo | Foxtrot | Golf | Hotel | India | Juliet | Kilo | Lima |

S is for SIERRA and SEAPLANE

Sierra is Spanish for a long jagged mountain chain. A Catalina seaplane was the first to fly from Australia to Valparaiso, by the rugged mountains of South America in 1951.

The Australian pilot was P. G. Taylor and his Catalina was named the Frigate Bird II. When he and his crew arrived at Easter Island to refuel, the sea was very rough. They landed on the lee side of the island, and to avoid his craft from being smashed into the cliffs by the sea, Taylor used his sailing skills to tack back.

Seaplanes do not require specially built runways because they land on smooth water anywhere. So they became first to fly the enormous distances across oceans and to circle the earth.

Luxurious flying boats flew passengers from Sydney to the holiday islands up until the 1970s. Seaplanes are still used as water bombers to fight fires over the vast expanses of Canada and Alaska – heroes till the end!

Oscar | Papa | Quebec | Romeo | Sierra | Tango

T is for TANGO and THRUST

Tango is a close dance where partners glide in unison. Thrust and lift are close partners in the dance of flight.

Thrust pushes aircraft forward. It may be provided by tiny engines in model planes or huge rockets that drive the Space Shuttle out of our protective atmosphere into space.

Thrust was a major problem to be solved before humans could fly. Aircraft engines need to be light, powerful, and reliable. Aircraft now fly three times the speed of sound and yet 100 years ago there was no engine suitable to power a plane into the air.

For the first fifty years of flight most designers chose radial engines. Since the 1950s jet turbines have evolved to function smoothly and with efficiency to create enormous power needed to push huge aircraft across the face of the earth.

The demands of this century will create new families of engines. Experimental engines burn hydrogen, and promise high speeds with little pollution. The main thrust will always be what we demand of our imagination to seek the best possible solutions.

1909 3-cylinder Anzani 19 kw

1908 Gnome Rotary 37 kw

1915 Mercedes 6-cylinder 120 kw

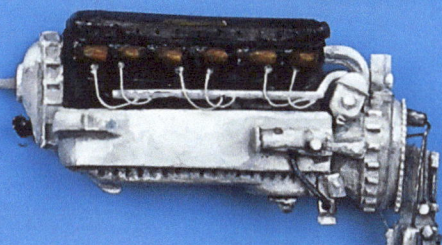

1942 Rolls Royce Merlin V12 1,340 kw

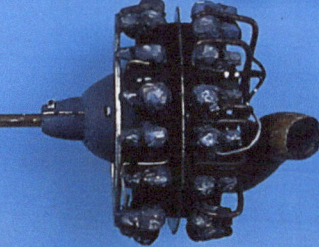

1949 Wright Turbo-Compound 2,586 kw

SNECMA Moteurs CFM56-5 31,200 to 34,000 pounds thrust

Alpha *Bravo* *Charlie* *Delta* *Echo* *Foxtrot* *Golf* *Hotel* *India* *Juliet* *Kilo* *Lima*

U *is for*
UNIFORM *and* UNDERCARRIAGE

Many people in aviation wear uniforms. A pilot's clothing is not the same as an engineer who checks the undercarriage.

The undercarrige is an attachment which aircraft use to land. They may be skis, skids, multiple and single wheels, or even large floats, depending on where
the aircraft is designed to operate. Russian planes often have mudguards to allow them to deal with rough airstrips.

Modern car tyres and powerful, light disc brakes with anti-lock systems are some of the innovations cars use today that were adapted from the undercarriage of aircraft.

The mighty Jumbo Jet uses a number of sets of wheels to spread the load when it lands. Smaller wheels take up less space in the aircraft so that more of the interior can be used for passengers, freight or fuel. It's a wonderful sight to watch all these wheels appear when such a large plane lands.

V is for VICTOR and VELOCITY

Victor is a man's name and also a word to describe a winner. Velocity is speed; something winners need.

In 1903 the Wright Flyer flew at barely 30 kilometres per hour, supported by the strong winds at Kill Devil Hills in North Carolina.

By 1945, fighter aircraft achieved over 850 kilometres in steep dives, an increase of over 800 kilometres per hour in forty years.

Aircraft such as the Concorde and the SR-71 in the 1960s far exceeded the speed of sound. Their engines developed huge amounts of power.

The wings were swept back sharply, the bodies were highly streamlined and they were built using special materials to insulate the interiors from the heat caused by the friction of the fast moving air.

The quest for speed has diminished as designers seek to make aircraft engines quieter, more economical and less polluting.

| Alpha | Bravo | Charlie | Delta | Echo | Foxtrot | Golf | Hotel | India | Juliet | Kilo | Lima |

| ber | Oscar | Papa | Quebec | Romeo | Sierra | Tango | Uniform | Victor | Whiskey |

W is for WHISKEY and WOMEN

A song mentions whiskey, a strong spirit, and wild women. Women pilots with strong spirits embarked on wild adventures.

Such spirit led Florence Taylor to be the first woman to fly a heavier-than-air craft in Australia when she launched from the dunes of Narabeen near Sydney in 1909.

From 1935 Nancy Bird earned a living flying people around the outback. She helped pioneer aerial medical services by flying nurses to outlying clinics.

Women became celebrities for daring flights. In the 1920s and 1930s, German Hanna Reitsch flew in gliding competitions, piloted the world's first practical helicopter, and tested the dangerous Me-163 rocket powered fighter.

Amazing women today have flown for the elite RAAF Roulettes aerobatic team, and become crew members on the awesome and complex F-111 fighter-bombers. They are a valued part of modern aviation.

Alpha | Bravo | Charlie | Delta | Echo | Foxtrot | Golf | Hotel | India | Juliet | Kilo | Lima

X is for
X-RAY and X-RAY CRACK TESTING

X-Rays are used to see within objects. They allow technicians to peer into aircraft structures probing for tiny cracks or signs of stress.

Aeroplanes are subject to many forces and loads in flight. If you look at the wings of a large jet taking off you can see forces moving the wings up and down. Such stresses over time can lead to breakages that can cause the aircraft to crash.

An X-Ray is just one of the important tests designed to detect areas of weakness. This information allows designers to create stronger structures and discover the safe life of components.

Y is for YANKEE and YOU

Yankee is slang for an American.

The Wright Brothers showed what those Yankees could achieve by solving the problems that had prevented people from making reliable aircraft.

Scientists study flying insects, hoping their secrets will inspire exciting new flying machines. Ultra-lightweight aircraft with tiny engines fly high above Earth researching our atmosphere. In time they may replace satellites, which would be much cheaper than using tonnes of rocket fuel to send heavy objects into space. It would also cause much less pollution. Small aircraft built for the exploration of Mars will send back pictures of the planet.

To make engines function in the Martian atmosphere, new technology and imagination will be needed to generate solutions. What could you achieve if you set your mind to it?

| Alpha | Bravo | Charlie | Delta | Echo | Foxtrot | Golf | Hotel | India | Juliet | Kilo | Lima |

Z is for ZULU and ZERO

Zulus are a tribe of formidable African fighters. Zero was the code name given to a fast, manoeuvrable Japanese fighter plane that ruled the skies above the Pacific early in World War II. Zeroes flew enormous distances by carrying external fuel tanks and they could be launched from aircraft carriers far from a battle. Allied aircraft of the time were no match for the Zero. It indicated the growing excellence of Japanese technology.

GLOSSARY

Avionics
A combination of the words aviation and electronics. It refers to all electronic-based instruments in an aircraft

Concorde
Supersonic airliner, jointly developed by France and England. Withdrawn 2003

Glass Screen
Fully electronic instrument display system

Global Positioning System
Very precise satellite-based system that informs users of their exact location

Gyroscope
Powered instrument based on a spinning disc, used in aircraft instruments for stability and accuracy

Kangaroo Route
Name for the first service between Australia and England, flown entirely by QANTAS using Lockheed Constellations

Lift
Force that causes an object to rise

Mach 1
The speed of sound is known as Mach 1. This varies according to the height and the temperature in which an aircraft travels. At sea level it is 1,225 kph, and at 6,00 metres it is approximately 1,000 kph

NATO
Northern Atlantic Treaty Organisation

Safe Life
The lifetime of a component recommended by the manufacturer

Scramjet Engine
Stands for Supersonic Combustion Ramjet. Unlike a rocket motor that carries oxygen for combustion, the Scramjet uses air moving into the intake at supersonic speed

Subsonic
Below the speed of sound

Supersonic
Above the speed of sound

WWI
World War One 1914 to 1918

WWII
World War Two 1939 to 1945

Zero
Originally A6M Fighter, in production became known as the Navy Type 0 Carrier Fighter

ILLUSTRATION REFERENCES & WHERE TO SEE AIRCRAFT

A is for Alpha
Boomerangs:
Museum Victoria, North Carlton, Vic.
Not attributable to known tribal groups

C is for Charlie
Vickers Vimy G-EAOU:
Adelaide International Airport,
West Beach, S.A.

D is for Delta
Inspired by hanging pterodactyl,
Museum Victoria, North Carlton, Vic.

F is for Foxtrot
Explore Royal Flying Doctor Service on:
www.flyingdoctor.net

G is for Golf
Hargrave Box kite replica:
Questacon, Canberra, A.C.T.

H is for Hazards
Flight data recorder prototype:
at Museum Victoria, North Carlton, Vic.
(in storage)

I is for India
Instrument panel, Sopwith Pup replica:
RAAF Air Museum, Point Cook Vic.

K is for Kilo
Fokker F VIIb-3m Kingsford Smith's
Southern Cross: Brisbane Airport, Qld.;
Southern Cross Replica: Southern Cross
Replica Association, Hanger 59, Parafield
Airport, S.A.

L is for Lima
Lockheed Hercules:
RAAF Museum, Point Cook, Vic.;
RAAF Base, Richmond, N.S.W.

M is for Mike
MiG-15:
Australian War Memorial, Canberra, A.C.T.;
P-51 Mustang:
Australian War Memorial, Canberra, A.C.T.;
Caboolture Warplane & Flight Heritage
Museum, Caboolture, Qld; Panama Jack's
Vintage Aircraft Company, Channing
Bridge, W.A.

N is for November
FA-18 RAAF Base, Tindal, Northern
Territory; FA-18 RAAF Base, Williamtown,
N.S.W.; Bert Hinkler, AVRO Avian:
Queensland Museum, Brisbane, Qld.

P is for Papa
F-111 RAAF Base, Amberley, Qld

Q is for Quebec
AVRO 504K & Boeing 747:
QANTAS Founders' Outback Museum,
Longreach, Qld.

R is for Racing
DC-2: Albury Airport, N.S.W.;
DC-3: Air Nostalgia, Essendon Airport,
Melbourne Vic. (flights available);
RAAF Association Aviation Heritage
Museum of Western Australia, Bull Creek,
W.A.; New Zealand Warbirds Association,
Ardmore, Auckland, New Zealand.

S is for Seaplane
Catalina: Powerhouse Museum, Sydney,
N.S.W.; RAAF Air Museum, Point Cook Vic.

T is for Thrust
Anzani 3 cylinder Bleriot XI replica:
Queen Victoria Museum, Launceston, Tas.;
Gnome Rotary Avro 504K: RAAF Air
Museum, Point Cook Vic. (oldest airbase
in Australia.); Mercedes 6: Australian War
Memorial, Canberra, A.C.T.

W is for Women
1909 Taylor Glider reproduction:
The Australian Aviation Museum, Bankstown,
N.S.W.; PC-9: RAAF Base, Central Flying
School, East Sale, Vic. Roulettes, RAAF Base,
Pearce, W.A.; Me 163b Komet: Australian War
Memorial, Canberra, A.C.T.

Y is for You
Pink bug: Based on micro-air vehicles,
www.ctie.monash.edu.au/hargrave/legacy1.
html

Z is for Zero
Mitsubishi A6M: Australian Aviation
Heritage, Winnellie, N.T.; Australian War
Memorial, Canberra, A.C.T.

Back cover:
Albatross D.Va:
Australian War Memorial, Canberra, A.C.T.

www.ingramcontent.com/pod-product-compliance
Lightning Source LLC
Chambersburg PA
CBHW041202290426
44109CB00002B/103